George A. Leavitt and Co.

Engravings, Etchings, Views and Illustrations, Ancient and Modern

George A. Leavitt and Co.

Engravings, Etchings, Views and Illustrations, Ancient and Modern

ISBN/EAN: 9783744702294

Printed in Europe, USA, Canada, Australia, Japan

Cover: Foto ©Thomas Meinert / pixelio.de

More available books at **www.hansebooks.com**

Engravings, Etchings, Views and Illustrations, Ancient and Modern.

A Large Collection of Plates, including choice examples of Old Masters, Subjects suitable for Framing, examples of Great Artists, Portraits, French Etchings, Miscellaneous Illustrations, Gallery Subjects, &c., some very fine Specimens of Sir Robert Strange, and a large variety of Subjects of the Modern School, Proofs on India Paper; examples of Turner, Stanfield, &c.

The whole to be sold by Auction at

CLINTON HALL,

Thursday, March 21st, and following days,
At 7½ P. M.

The Messrs. LEAVITT, Auctioneers.

CATALOGUE.

1 SCULPTURE Illus. the History of France.   43.

2 DRAMATIC French Portraits, Mrs. Mante, Duches-
nois, Minette, etc.   17.

3 VIEWS Illus. the History of France.   50.

4 PHILLIBROWN, The Truant, India proof, Smith,
David brought before Saul, proof, etc.   3.

5 HEATH, The Attack, Kernot, Waiting for the
Boats, India proof, etc.   8.

6 COUSEN, Rest in the Desert, Ratcliffe, Morning
on the Sea Coast, etc.   8.

7 OUTRIM, The Dancing Lesson, India proof, Finden,
The Cherry Sellers, etc.   3.

8 ALLEN, The Columns of St. Mark Venice, Taylor,
Red Cap, etc.   4.

9 LANGSTER, The Victim, The Challenge, fine India
proofs before letters.   2.

10 ALLEN, Temple of Jupiter Panhellenius, Stocks,
Apollo Killing the Python, etc.   8.

11 GOODELL. The Poor Soldier, Greatback, Raffle
for a Watch. Fine India proofs before letter.   2.

12 CORREGGIO, Ecce Homo, Splendid line Engraving by Geo. T. Doo. Brilliant impression.   1.

13 NORRISON, King James and his Jeweller, George
Heriot, fine impression.   1.

14 BOCCACCIO's DECAMERON, Calandrina, Bruno, and
Buffatinacca, Philips, Duke and Duchess reading Don Quixote, fine.   2.

15 HATFIELD, The Reduced Gentleman's Daughter,
Allen, a Battle Scene, India proof before letters.   2.

16 PORTRAITS Illustrating the History of France.　　50.

17 ALLEN, Lady Godiva, Bell, The Bagpiper, India proofs.　　2.

18 KNIGHT, The Death of Cardinal Wolsey, Baralet, Tom Jones fall from a Tree.　　2.

19 LANDSEER, High Life, proof before letter very fine.　　1.

20 CRALL, The Tired Soldier, Brandard, The Stepping Stone, India proofs, etc.　　3.

21 TAYLOR, Reading the News, Greatback, the First Ear-Ring, India proofs.　　2.

22 HAMILTON, The Antient English Wake, Egan, A Covenanter, etc.　　3.

23 VIEWS Illustrating the Hist. of France.　　50.

24 STORM, Portrait of Shakspeare, Do. by Hall, India proof, scarce.　　2.

25 SHAKSPEARE before Sir Thomas Lucy, Shakspeare's Birth Place, proof, scarce.　　2.

26 ROMNEY, Shakspeare, Troilus and Cressida, Graham, Othello, fine, folio.　　2.

27 SMIRKE, Shakspeare Measure for Measure, Portrait of Shakspeare, proof before letters.　　2.

28 WHEATLEY, Shakspeare, Tempest, Say, Queen Mab.　　2.

29 DIGAGE, Die Wasserteitung, Aqueduc, Temple de Minerve D'Apollon, Murcure, etc.　　7.

30 BUCK, Powderham Castle, the Seat of the Earl of Devon, Scott, German tunes, etc.　　15.

31 LAMBERT & Scott, Views of Plymouth and Mount Edgcumbe.　　5.

32 GUTTENBERG, Vue de la Suisse, Ouvrier, Vue des Alpes, etc.　　5.

33 GAINSBOROUGH, Land-Guard, Fort Suffolk, Chesham, mouth of the Coal Pit, Shropshire, etc.　　3.

34 WESTALL, Warwick Castle, Sullivan, Witten the Seat of Earl Pembroke, etc.　　6.

35 CLAUDE LORAIN, View on the River Po, in Italy Fine line engraving, good impression.　　1.

36 JUKES, View of the Fountain of Egeria near Rome, Dunker, Vue de Livourne.　　5.

37 SHULBACH, Vue du Nord Est d Athenes Dunker, Vue de Livourne, etc. 7.

38 HACKERT, Porto D'Ancona, Villa D'Este, Porto di Toranto, etc. 6.

39 LORD WILLIAM RUSSELL 1683, Godfrey, The Council of War at Courtray. India paper, etc. 8.

40 COUSEN, The old Pier at Littlehampton, The Battle of Trafalgar. Fine India proof line engravings. 3.

41 GREATBACH. The Raffle for the Watch, Smyth, The Last In. Fine India proofs. 2.

42 ARTLETT. The Countess, Wagner, The Flower Girl. Proofs. 2.

43 SHARPE, The Peep O Day Boys Cabin, Shenton, Country Cousins. 2.

44 VIEWS Illustrating the History of France. 50.

45 TRAMMEL, Aetna, Schrœder, Views in Hessen Cassel, etc. 7.

46 CLAUDE Lorain, Vue des Edifices de Rome, Elliott, View of Tivoli, etc. Fine line. 3.

47 DUNKER and Smelin, Views in Tivoli, etc. 8.

48 THE FAIR SLEEPER, The Dangerous Playmate. India proofs. 2.

49 JEENS, The Summer Gift, Stocks, The Vintage in the South France. India proof. 2.

50 VIEWS in Rome, Germany, etc., some in colors. 18.

51 JUKES, View of the Subterraneous Ruins of Mercenas's Villa Tivoli, Hackert, Views of Pompei, etc. 15.

52 HACKERT, Veduta di Pozzuali, Vue de Caserte, etc. 10.

53 ROD, Vue du Rhin a Lauffenbourg after Smelin fine line engraving. 1.

54 CRAYONS by F. Boucher. 6.

55 STUDIES by Boucher nude subjects, etc. 5.

56 TURNER, Approach to Venice, very fine India proof. 1.

57 TURNER, Rain, Steam and Speed, very fine India proof. 1.

58 TURNER, Snow Storm, very fine India proof. 1.
59 TURNER, Line Fishing off Hastings, very fine India proof. 1.
60 TURNER, Venice. The Bridge of Sighs, very fine India proof. 1.
61 TURNER. The Prince of Orange Landing at Torbay, very fine India proof. 1.
62 TURNER. Wreck off Hastings, very fine India proof. 1.
63 TURNER, Heidelberg, very fine India proof. 1.
64 HALL, Portrait of J. M. W. Turner, very fine India proof. 1.
65 TURNER, The Fighting Temeraire, very fine India proof. 1.
66 GOODALL, Westminster Abbey and Bridge, proof. 1.
67 PORTRAIT of Pope Clemens XIII, etc. 2.
68 TURNER, The Goddess of Discord. 1.
69 TURNER, The Birdcage, Bacchus and Arcadne, India proofs. 2.
70 STUDIES by Boucher. 5.
71 THE Tambourine, The Brides of Venice, India proofs. 2.
72 STUDIES by Boucher. 5.
73 OUTRIM, Christ Lamenting over Jerusalem, Challis, A Jewish Synagogue, India proofs. 2.
74 HACKERT, Views of Pompei, et de Persano, etc. 9.
75 BRITISH Coins, by Landseer, Thompson, etc. 10.
76 BRITISH and Roman Coins, by Newton, Roffe, etc. 10.
77 BROMLEY, Prints Illustrating the Hist. of England. 11.
78 BROMLEY, Prints Illus. the History of England. 11.
79 TURNER, On the Thames, Phryne going to the Bath as Venus, India proofs. 2.
80 TURNER, Blight Sand, Apollo killing the Python, India proofs. 2.
81 TURNER, The Golden Bough, Frosty Morning Sunrise, India proofs. 2.
82 TURNER, Caligula's Palace and Bridge, Dido and Aneas, India proofs. 2.

84 Bromley, Prints Illus. the History of England. 11.

85 Dunker, Vue de Cantalupo et Bardella anc Mandela, et Vue de Fonte Bella, etc. 26.

86 Turner, Apollo and Daphne in the Vale of Tempe, Child Harold's Pilgrimage, Italy, India proofs. 2.

87 Canalleffi Venise, Vue en Tirol, etc. 5.

88 Bromley, Prints Illus. the History of England. 11.

89 Bromley, Prints Illus. the History of England. 11.

90 Strutt, Vues de la Baviere, colored. 1.

91 Turner, Dutch Boats in a Gale, Modern Italy, India proofs. 2.

92 Dramatic Portraits, M. J. Proctor, M. Cooke. 2.

94 Dramatic Portraits, Mlle. Cileste, Miss Fanny Wyndham. 2.

95 Dramatic Portrait, Miss Sydney, proof and Malibran. 2.

96 Dramatic Portraits, Mr. Kean, Miss Woolgar. 2.

97 Dramatic Portraits Mlle. Taglioni, Mars, Amalia Halend. 8.

98 Dramatic French Portraits, Mlle. Jawurck, Taglioni. 2.

99 Dramatic French Portraits, Mme. Malibran, proof Mlle. Rancourt. 2.

100 Dramatic Portraits, Mme. Eckerlin, Mlle. Nablet, colored. 2.

101 Dramatic Portraits, Ludewig Devrient, Mr. Wieland. 2.

102 Dramatic Portraits, Anne le Fevre, Dacier, Henriette Sontag, etc. 8.

103 Dramatic Portraits, M. II. Betty, Giacinto Murras, etc. 3.

104 Illustrations to Shakespeare, by Smirke. 20.

105 Illustrations to Shakespeare, by Smirke, Westall, etc. 20.

106 Illustrations to Shakespeare, by Smirke, proofs. 20.

107 Illustrations to Shakespeare, by Westall, Hamilton, etc. 20.

108 ILLUSTRATIONS to Shakespeare, by Stothard, Ibet-
son, Mortimers Etchings, India proofs.   20.
109 PATER, Fete Campetre, Stanfield, Castle of Ischia,
India proofs.   2.
110 WILD BOAR Hunting, Wonvermans, Pferdestall,
etc.   6.
111 WOUVERMANS, Sleighing, Letters from Mimic
Gallery.   6.
112 ILLUSTRATIONS to Shakespeare, by Hamilton,
Wheatley, etc.   20.
113 HOLBEIN, Barbara, Carl Dolce, St. Magdalena, etc.   6.
114 ADRIAN van Ostade, Kinder Verkaufen Obst after
Murilla, etc. Fine litho's from the Dresden
Gallery.   6.
115 VANDYCK, Jupiter and Io, Carraccio, litho's from
the Dresden and Munich Galleries.   6.
116 HEIL Jungfreau, Ein Faun und Eine Nymphe,
after Tizian, etc.   6.
117 WINTER Scene in Holland, Ponte Lupo Tivoli,
etc.   6.
118 GIRARD, Rosane, the Mistress of Alexander.   1.
119 ILLUSTRATIONS to Shakespeare, by Stothard, Miller,
etc.   20.
120 ORIGINAL Studies by French Academies Students
from Life and from Casts.   7.
121 HOLT, The Rustic Toilet, Aubert, Nelly, etc.   3.
122 POILLY, Holy Family, fine line engraving.   1.
123 SABAT, after Tenier, line engraving.   1.
124 LIGHTFOOT, Arming the Young Knight, etc.
India proofs.   2.
125 RICHARDSON, Æneas Landing in Italy, proof before letters, Bourne, The Butt Shooting a
Cherry, etc.   8.
126 WILLMORE, The Battle of Waterloo, Miller,
Claude, Landscape, etc. Fine.   3.
127 ALLEN, Trent in the Tyrol, Friederichi, etc.   3.
128 JEENS, The Controversy, Greatbach, The Break-
fast Table, etc. India proofs.   3.
129 SMITH, an Italian Family, in the Sepulchre.
Proofs, etc.   8.

130 **HEATH**, The Lesson of the Passover, Lemon, Left in Charge. Proofs, etc. 8.
131 **ETCHINGS** by Boret, You, Durjan etc. 6.
132 **ETCHINGS** by Perrin, Etienne, Chauvel, etc. 6.
133 **ETCHINGS** by Monzier, Montbard, etc., India proofs. 5.
134 **ETCHINGS** by Courtry, Bracquemond, Flameng, etc., superb India proofs. 5.
135 **EPPOMNA** after West, Roma, Forum Romain, etc. 6.
136 **ETCHINGS** by Martin, Balfourier, etc. 5.
137 **ETCHINGS** by Duran, Roybet,Nitti, etc., India proofs. 4.
138 **ETCHINGS** by Hoybet, Boland, P. Potter, Groscilliez. 4
139 **STUDIES** by Boucher. 6.
140 **VIEWS** Illustrating the History of France. 50.
141 **LES PATINEURS** after Ostade, Portrait de Deus Jeunes Gens, etc. 8.
142 **ILLUSTRATIONS** to Shakespeare, by Westall, Walker, etc. 20.
143 **JESUS**, Portant sa Crais, Une Lettre de France, etc. 6.
144 **THE GRACES**, after Rubens, Rellet, L'Africaine Hospitalier, etc. 4.
145 **DIANE** et Endymion, Aquila, Vergine, etc. 5.
146 **WOUVERMANS**, Battles, etc., finely engraved by Moyreau. 4.
147 **RELIGIONE** after Raphael by Corichi. 1.
148 **CAMERATA**, David with Head of Goliah after Farelli, fine. 1.
149 **FINE** Etchings by Bartolozzi, after Guercino. 8.
150 **ETCHINGS** by Bartolozzi after Guercino. 8.
151 **BALSWORTH**, Landscapes after Rubens, fine. 3.
152 **PHILLIPS**, The Studious Philospher, after Rembrandt, fine. 1.
153 **POILLY**, St. John, very fine. 1.
154 **FALO**, Dianna, very fine line engraving. 1.
155 **RADIGUES**, Angelica, fine line engraving. 1.
156 **ETCHING**, by Rahl, fine. 1.
157 **BETRAYAL** of Christ, unfinished, fine engraving. 1.
158 **CONTARDE**, Classical Subjects, fine line engravings. 2.

159 GIOVANNI Falo, Gallatea, fine line engraving. 1.

160 LANRENT Le Pacage Hollaindaise after Paul Potter, Le Triomphe De LAmour, etc. 3.

161 BADAS, Paul testifying to the Jews that Jesus is the Christ, after Govanni. 1.

162 LEMPEREUR, Le Triomphe de Silene after Vanloo, very fine. 1.

163 PORTRAITS of the Earl of Albermarle, Binda Attovitii, James Stuart, proof, etc. 4.

164 VIRGIN and Child and St. John, proof before letters by Gaudolfi. 1.

165 DANTTE, Le Prix de la Beaute, very fine. 1.

166 BOYDELL, Nero depositing the Ashes of Britannicus, The Judgment of Midas, colored. 2.

167 RICCIANI, fine engraving after Guido, Dead Christ and Mary. 1.

168 LONGUEIT, Les Madeles, fine. 1.

169 REYNOLDS, Robin Gray, Madonna and Child, proofs before letters. 2.

170 PORTRAITS by Turner, R. Duppa, Coke Watts. 3.

171 PORTRAITS, Turner, Lord Listal, India proof, H. C. Combe M. P., H. W. Longfellow. 3.

172 PORTRAITS, The Pope etc. After Lawrence, some proofs before letter. 3.

173 PORTRAITS, after Reynolds, etc., Taylor, Lord, Teignmouth. 2.

174 BARTOLOZZI, Andrew Kippis, etc., some proofs before letter, finely engraved. 3.

175 LIGHTFOOT, The Orphan, India Proof. 1.

176 HEATH, Alic Lisle, Cousen, Calais Pier, Crossing the Brook, proofs. 3.

177 CHEMIN, Creux colored, Amor seinen Gladnen, etc. 3.

178 JUKES, Views on the River Wye, Chepstow Castle and Bridge, Redbrook, etc. 7.

179 BARTOLOZZI, Subjects after Guercini. 4.

180 LIZARS, The Scribes reading the Chronicle to Ahasuerus, Cousens, The Fountain, India proofs. 2.

9

2

203 GALLE, The Resurrection, and The Last Supper, fine, etc. 4.

204 COUSINET, Les Suites D'un Naufrage, Balswert, Landscape, after Rubens etc. 3.

205 EVE, St. Catharine, proof fine. 1.

206 GILLER, Fighting for the Standard, Rest, The Parting etc. 5.

207 COCHIN, Vene de Tournay, very fine. 1.

208 POUSSIN, Le Matin, Le Campanile anc Mons Lucretilis, etc. 4.

209 AUDRAN, fine Cupid and Psyche, fine engraved. 1.

210 TOMKINS, Portrait of Governor Eyre of Jamaica, fine India proof, etc. 4.

211 VISSCHER, The Travelling Musicians after Ostade, fine and rare. 1.

212 LEONIDAS King of Sparta, after Sir B. West in colors. 1.

213 VIRGO cum Puero after Raphael, splendid engraving by Folo, fine impression. 1.

214 MICHEL, Abraham, Sarah and Hagar, after Guido and Cortona. 3.

215 AUDRAN, Le Centaure nesse enleve de Janire, Kruger, La Mort de Clorinde. 2.

216 VEAU, Vue des Environs de Bayonne, Daulle, Les Tendres Adieux de la Laitiere, etc. 8.

217 GREEN, Queen Philippa soliciting for the lives of the Citizens of Calais, very fine mezzotint. 1.

218 VIEWS, Illustrating the History of France. 50.

219 SMIRKE, Illustrations to Shakespeare mostly proofs. 20.

220 THE Motherly Fright after Schott, Le Roman, after Pages, fine impressions. 2.

221 RENI, Loth, La Jaconde, after Leonardi de Vinci, etc. 8.

222 VAN DYCK, Taking down from the Cross, fine impression before letter, Bolsurst. 1.

223 BOAR Hunting after Rubens, Elliott, View of the Intendant's Palace, etc. 8.

224 GOODALL, The Piper, very fine. 1.

225 MILLER, Loch Au-Eilan, fine. 1.

226 OBITUS, S. Cæciliæ Virginis et Martyris, after
Domenichio, Johannes est nomem eius, after
Sarto, etc.   6.

227 LEMPEREUR, La Sortie du Bain.   1.

228 THE death of Lucrece, finely engraved by Cathelin,
after Pellegrini, The Tomtit, after Dulufe.   2.

229 VASSEUR, La Mort D'Adonis, after Boucher, fine.   1.

230 THE Head of John Baptist, etc., finely engraved
after Guercino, brilliant impression.   1.

231 VIEW in Andalusia Henriquas, Sainte Famille,
fine.   2.

232 SHENTON, The Clemency of Cœur-de-Lion, very
fine.   1.

233 WICAR, Antiques, Gems from the Florence Gallery.
These little Gems exhibit most exquisite designs
and engravings of the human figure, and can
only be obtained by the destruction of a copy
of the Florence Gallery.   11.

234 WICAR, Antiques Gems, fine.   10.

335 WICAR, Antiques Gems, fine.   10.

236 WICAR, Antiques Gems, fine.   10.

237 WICAR, Antiques Gems, fine.   10.

238 WICAR, Antiques Gems, fine.   10.

239 ILLUSTRATIONS to Shakespeare, Northcote, Porter,
etc.   20.

240 ILLUSTRATIONS to Shakespeare, by Smirke, Walker,
etc.   13.

241 BROMLEY, Prints Illustrating the History of England.   13.

242 BEGA, Le Joueur de Guitare, Berghem, Passage,
etc., from Florence Gallery.   9.

243 A SELECTION of fine pieces, Brilliant Impressions,
from the Florence Gallery.   14.

244 SELECTION of Subjects from the Orleans Gallery,
on copper.   7.

245 WICAR, Antiques, Gems, Florence Gallery.   9.

246 LE BRUN, Zampieri, etc., Subjects from the Orleans Gallery.   6.

247 MOUCHERON, La Chute D'Eau, Carrache, Le Bate-
lier, etc.   8.

248 CARRACHE, Les Chasseurs, Miel, La Vendange,
etc.   11.

249 RUBENS, Continence de Scipion, Romain, La
Nouriture D'Hercule, etc.   7.

250 TENIERS, La Fumense, Rubens, L'Adventure de
Philopœmen, etc.   9.

251 VIEWS in London, Public Buildings, etc.   101.

252 AMERICAN Indians, colored painted from life, Mc-
Kinney and Hall.   6.

253 AMERICAN Indians, colored by hand, folio.   6.

254 AMERICAN Indians, colored by hand.   6.

255 AMERICAN Indians, colored.   6.

256 VIEWS Illustrating the History of France.   50.

257 JEENS, Drift Wreck from the Armada, Bourne,
The Fair Correspondent, India proofs.   2.

258 COUSEN, The Height of Ambition, Goodall, The
Post Boy, India proofs.   2.

259 GREATBACH, Accident or Design, Jacob Chez
Laban after Murillo, etc.   3.

260 COUSENS, The Sabbath Eve, Lightfoot, The Way-
farers, India proofs.   2.

261 MARE, The Negligent Boy, Bourne, New Shoes,
India proofs, etc.   3.

262 FINDEN, The Harvest Wagon, Greatbach, The
Claim for Shelter, etc.   3.

263 JEENS, The Controversy, Lightfoot, The Foundling, India proof.   2.

264 CHATELAIN, La Devidense Italienne, Jazet, Le
Loup et L'Agneau.   2.

265 ROBERTS, Italian Scenery, proof, St. Johns Church
Windsor.   2.

266 S. CATHARINA, Poilly, La Sainte Vierge adorant
l'Enfant Jesus, etc.   4.

267 MECON, Ne Mange pas Tout, Queen of Beauty,
etc.   8.

268 WILLMORE, In Old Hyde Park, India proof, Whit-
field, Finding the Body of Harold, etc.   3.

269 L'ABREUVAIR, Les Deux Montagnes, Pieces from
Orleans Gallery.   9.

270 GUIDO, S. Hieronymus, Galatea after Carracci, etc., all fine impressions. 3.

271 VECELLI, Diane et Calista, Rubens, Les Suites de la Guerre, etc. 6.

272 CATLIN, Buffalo Hunt, Coloured Indian Scenes, etc. Folio. 4.

273 CANOT, View of the Harbour of the Havana, etc. 2.

274 RAPE of Proserpine, Poussin, Bacchus, etc., from Orleans Gallery. 9.

275 CATLIN, American Indians at their Games, Dances, etc. Coloured. 6.

276 PORTRAITS of Marie Antoinette, Mary de Medicis, Christina of Sweden, etc. 7

277 RENI, Portraits of Catherine of Russia, Beatrix Cenci, Anna Boleyn, etc. 6.

278 DARNER, Bayrischen Hachgebirge, Wynnuts, Landschaft, etc. 6.

279 VAN DYCK, Marquis de Mirabelle, Tiziau, Peter Aretin, etc. 6.

280 ECCE HOMO, Holy Family, Assention of Maria, etc. 6.

281 ROMEYN, Rubens, etc., from Munich Gallery. 6.

282 MIERIS, Femme de Fois, finely engraved by Klauber. 1.

283 BOLSWERT, Landscape after Rubens. 1.

284 ANGELICA Kauffman, Telemachus at the Court of Sparta. 1.

285 VISSCHER, Andrea Adoni after Corregio. 1.

286 FRERET, Le Mariage des Negres, Bust and Coins, etc. 3.

287 RUGA, Piazza Colonna at Rome, Edridges, Portrait of Lord F. Campbell, etc. 4.

288 AUBERT, Siege de Maestricht, Boucher, Faire de Campagne, etc. 6.

289 WOUVERMANS, Les Chasseurs Sartant de la Forest, Poussin, L'Enlevement des Sabines, etc. 23.

290 BLOOTELING, Diana and the Nymps, Depart du Messager D'Armour. Scarce. 2.

291 GOODALL, Rural Scene, India Proof, Guido, La Magdelaine, etc.   4

292 ANCIENT Towns, Mauritus, Rio Grande, North Carolina, Nova Mexico, Olinda, fine impressions of rare old views, folio.   5.

293 ANCIENT Towns, Ars Massavii, St. Martin, Potasi, Porto Rico, Paraba, rare old views, folio.   5.

294 ANCIENT Towns, Vetus Mexico, Bonvista, Callao de Lima, St. Francisco, Truxillo, old views, rare, folio.   5.

295 ANCIENT Towns, Partus Acapulco, Partus Calvi Tamaraca, Cartagena.   4.

296 BERGHEM, Le Gue, Gindo, Virgin and Infant Jesus, etc.   4.

297 MASON, View of the Orphans or Useline Nunnery, Effigies of King John and Queen Phillippa, etc.   8.

298 Le BAS, La Fraiche Martinee, very fine.   1.

299 SHERWIN, Portrait of Sir Joshua Reynolds, India proof.   1.

300 ETCHINGS by Classin after Rembrandt and others, mounted on a sheet.   8.

301 SANDLY, View of Miramichi in the Gulf of St. Lawrence, Wouvermuns, Mache D'Armee, etc.   5.

302 WICAR, Antiques, Gems, from Florence Gallery.   10.

303 VERNON, The Virgin Mother, Franck, The Warriors Cradle, India proof, etc.   3.

304 WALLIS, The Bay of Naples Early Morning, Smith, View on the River Stour, etc.   3.

305 AMERICAN Indians, colored.   6.

306 BURNET, The Adoration, The Banished Lord, after Sir J. Reynolds.   2.

307 LIGHTFOOT, The Peril of the Queen Henrietta Maria, Goodall, Felice Ballarin reciting Tasso to the People of Chioggia, India proofs.   2.

308 GODFREY, The Defence of Lathom House, 1644, Franck Hush, He Sleeps, India proof, etc.   3.

309 VIEWS Illustrating the History of France.   50

310 PORTRAITS Illustrating the History of France.   50

311 AMERICAN Scenery on the Hudson.   15.

312 AMERICAN Scenery on the Hudson.   15.

313 BROMLEY, Prints Illustrating the History of England. 11.

314 BROMLEY, Prints Illustrating the History of England. 18.

315 BROMLEY, Prints Illustrating the History of England. 12.

316 CUYP, An Acquatic Fete at Dart. India proof, fine piece. 1.

317 MORGHEN, Infant, after Congie. India proof. 1.

318 BOLSWERT, Landscapes after Rubens, very fine and rare. 8.

319 WOUVERMANS, Le Travail du Marechal, Le Port au Foin. 2.

320 HEATH, Going Home, Goodall, The Swing. India proofs. 2.

321 OUTHWAITE, The Village Dance, Goodall, Hunt the Slipper, India proofs. 2.

322 STANCLIFFE, The Temptation of Andrew Marvell, Thevenin, The Skein Winders. India proofs. 2.

323 WICAR, Antiques, Gems, fine. 10.

324 LANDSEER, Sharp etc., Medallions of Royalty, Poets, etc., Illustrating English History. 10.

325 BROMLEY, Medallion Portraits Illustrating the History of England. 10.

326 WOUVERMANS, Le Passage de L'Eau, Bolswert, Landscape after Rubens, etc. 8.

327 GUTTENBURG, fine engraving, after Flink. 1.

328 PALMER, Juppiter et Antiopa, fine impression. 1.

329 NANTEUIL, Portrait of Van Steenberghen, fine. 1.

330 NANTEUIL, Portrait of Jacques Marquis de Castelnau, fine. 1.

331 GALLE, The Resurrection, Rembrandt, The Good Samaritan, etc. 8.

332 LANDSCAPE, after Galle, Les Souffleurs et le Paixan Credule. 2.

333 LENFANT, Portrait of J. L. de Guillard fine, good impression. 1.

334 RAPHAEL, Frederic duc D'Urbin Engraved by Langier. 1.

335 WILSON, Epponina after West, colored, etc. 2.
336 RUBENS, Faith, Hope and Charity, etc. 2.
337 ETCHING by Vissher, Landscape and Cattle, etc. on a sheet. 2.
338 MOCHETTI, Portrait of Pio Sexto, and Paul Potter, etc. 5.
339 VANLO, Porporati Clorinde et Tancrede. 1.
340 A GAME at Cards, a fine and valuable engraving, brilliant impression. 1.
341 WOUVERMANS, Poste pres D'Anvers fine. 1.
342 CALLCOTT, Benevolent Cottagers. 1.
343 PHILLIPS, Holy Family, unfinished proof. 1.
344 DELAUNAY, Clorinde et Tancrede. 1.
345 VAN DYCK, Portrait of Joannes de Wael, fine. 1.
346 STRANGE, Venus attired by the Graces, very fine. 1.
347 ANSDELL, Setter and Grouse. 1.
348 STRANGE, Robert, Cleopatra applying the Serpent to her bosom. 1.
349 STRANGE, Sir Robert, Cupid, very fine. 1.
350 STRANGE, Sir Robert, Cupid Sleeping, very fine and brilliant impression. 1.
351 STRANGE, Esther a Suppliant before Ahasuerus. 1.
352 STRANGE, Sir Robert, Joseph and Potiphar's Wife, very fine. 1.
353 STRANGE, Sir Robert, Cleopatra, full length, nude very fine. 1.
354 STRANGE, Apollo rewarding Merit and punishing Arrogance, very fine. 1.
355 STRANGE, Robert, Liberality and Modesty, very fine, nude figures. 1.
356 STRANGE, Sir Robert, the finding of Romulus and Remus, very fine. 1.
357 STRANGE, Belisarius, very fine impression. 1.
358 STRANGE, The Judgement of Hercules, very fine and choice impression. 1.
359 STRANGE, Venus attired by the Graces, very fine. 1.
360 PHILLIPS, The Guardian Angel, fine. 1.
361 BOLSWERT, Landscape after Rubens, very fine. 1.

362 Bolswert, Silenus, very fine. 1.
363 Bolswert, Landscape and Sea View, after Rubens, fine. 1.
364 Killan, Portrait of Francis I, fine. 1.
365 Kauffman, Vortigern and Rowena, fine. 1.
366 Masson, Portrait of Comes de Crecy, fine. 1.
367 Marchand, Martens Scevola before Porsenna, very fine. 1.
368 Rubens, The Holy Family, Lorain Marine, etc. 7.
369 Bartolozzi, Departure of Mary Queen of Scots to France when a Child, etc. 5.
370 Saxon, Roman and Baitish Coins, by Walker, Multon, etc. 10.
371 Portraits Illustrating the History of France. 43.
372 Sculpture, Illustrating the History of France. 45.
373 Landseer, Neale, etc. Medallions of Antiquaries, Nobles, Poets, etc., Illustrating English History. 10.
374 Poussin, Le Soir, Watteau, Promenade sur les Remparts in Munimenta Deanabulatia, etc. 8.
375 Le Brun, La Pais Ramene L'Abondance, etc. 8.
376 Lawrence, Portrait of Sir Humphrey Davy. 1.
377 Greatbach, Courtship by the Sea Side, Goodall, Felice Ballariu RecitingTasso to the People of Chiuggia. India proofs. 2.
378 Lightfoot, The Sabbath Eve, The Foundling. India proofs. 2.
379 Jeen, the Justice of the King, Heath, The Lesson of the Passover. India proofs. 2.
320 Armytage, The Cavalier, India Proof, Robinson, The Spanish Flower Girl, etc. 8.
381 Lorenzi, Marriage of St. Catherine, Tombleson, Vue des Environs de Geneve, etc. 6.
382 Caracci, Susanna and the Elders, Sea View after Lorraine. Proof, etc. 8.
383 Lawrence, Portrait of the Duke of Wellington. Fine. 1.
384 Aubert, Vue Prise dans L'Andalousie, Mongeal, Portrait de dena Jennes Gens, etc. 4.

3

385 Jacquand, Laurence dans la Grotte des aigles, fine impression. 1.

386 Curious Portrait of Henry Robinson, Bishop of Carlisle, Christ Agony in the Garden after Rubens, etc. 4.

387 Galle, Holy Family, The Graces, after Rubens. Fine. 2.

388 Murillo, Lutte de Jacob, Poussin, L'Assomption de la Vierge, etc. 5.

389 Poussin, Meeting of Abraham and Rebecca, Legrand, Remontrances du Cure, etc. 8.

390 Le Mire, La Grande Rade Hollandoise. Fine. 1.

391 Smirke, Landseer, etc., Medallions of Divines, Nobles, etc., Illustrating English History. 10.

392 Bartolomeo, Presentation in Temple, Vanbalein, Mariage de la Vierge, etc. 10.

393 Cigale, Descente de Croix, Mercandini, Visitation de la Vierge, etc. 9.

394 Statuary Antiques, by Wicar, fine. 12.

395 American Indians, colored. 6.

396 American Indians, colored. 6.

397 American Indians, colored. 6.

398 American Indians, colored. 6.

399 Andran, Les Pelerins D'Emmans, Harbours and Fortifications of Cronstadt, etc. 4.

400 Elliott, Town and Harbour of Sanzon, Van Velde, Le Point du Jour, etc. 6.

401 Shaw, Falls of St. Anthony on the Mississippi, Le Lace de Geneve a Vevey, etc. 6.

402 Scriven, Gerard Dow, India proof. 1.

403 Schmuzer, Vlysse Enlevant le fils D'Andromaque, fine impression. 1.

404 Laurent, Le Passage du Rhin, Berghem, Le Retour au Hameau, etc. 11.

405 Alban, At Phaeton rutilos flamma populante capillas, very fine line engravings. 1.

406 Hackert, Veduta del Parto dell Isola D'Ischia, Veduta di Marechiano oppresso Pasilipo a Napoli, etc. 6.

407 HACKERT, Avanzi del Tempio di Giove Serapide
a Pozzuoli, etc. 12.

408 WOUVERMANS, L'Abrenvoir, very fine. 1.

409 CUYPE. The Contented Peasants, 'fine, Shaw,
Bolling's Dam, Petersburgh, Virginia, etc. 13.

410 VERNET, Incendie Nocturne, Valentin, Le Denier
de Cesar, etc. 3.

411 WOUVERMANS, Hatte D'Oficiers, fine. 1.

412 BAILLARDI, The Maries at the Tomb, Christ ap-
pearce to Mary, after Raphael, etc. 3.

413 NOUAL, View of Bethlehem, Pennsylvania, Wouvermans, Course de la Bagne, etc. 8.

414 BARON, Jupiter amoureux d'Antiope se trans-
forme en Satire, very fine. 1.

415 VALLEE, Resurrection du Lazarre, Desplaces,
Marcus Curtius, etc. 7.

416 JEAURAT, Repos en Egypte, Harthemcls, Naissance
de St. Jean, etc. 3.

417 VAN DYCK, Mænul Bildniss, Rubens, Helena For-
man, etc. 6.

418 A. DURER, The Crucifixion, Raphael, Taking
down from the Cross, etc. 6.

419 PORTRAITS Illustrating the History of France. 50.

420 POILLY, Nativite de Jesus Christ, Raymond, Les
Israelites recuillans la Manne, etc., fine. 4.

421 BROMLEY, Prints Illus. the History of England. 13.

422 ROMAIN, Apollon et les Muses, Wicar, Bas Relief
Antique, ete. 9.

423 GUIBERTI, Triomphe D'Ariadne, Corado, Arthe-
mise, etc. 9.

424 STATUARY Antiques and Bas-Relief, by Wicar,
fine, from the Florence Gallery. 11.

425 STUDIES by Boucher. 6.

426 BOURNE, The Crown of Hops, Children, India
proof before letters. 2.

427 SANGSTER, A Syrian Maid, Robinson, The Spanish
Flower Girl, India proof. 2.

428 HEATH, The First Voyage, Kernot, Waiting for
the Boats, India proofs. 2.

429 DESPLACES L'Amour heurewx, Vallee, Moyse trouve sur le Nil, etc. 7.

430 MACENAY, La Fleuriste, fine. 1.

431 YUKES, Views in the Canton of Glarus Swisserland, etc. 11.

432 DANZEL, Neptune et Amymone, Ala Santa du Roi, etc. 3.

433 GERANT, Femme Accrochant une Volaille, Forster, Jeune Femme a sa Fenétre, etc. 4.

434 BOLSWERT, Silenus after Van Dyck, very fine. 1.

435 GUIDO, Ecce Homo, fine impression of Lignons celebrated engraving. 1.

436 LEWIS, Portrait of Lord Byron, very fine. 1.

437 WALKER, Portrait of Sir Walter Scott, finest portrait of Scott, after Raeburn. 1.

438 CARRACHE, La Sainte Famille, Pontius, Crucifixion, fine, etc. 3.

439 DANZEL, Le Gateau des Rois, Bartolozzi and Browne, Europa. 2.

440 JORDANS, Recreatian de la Table, fine. 1.

441 BROMLEY, Prints Illustrating the History of England. 11.

442 BROMLEY, Prints Illustrating the History of England. 11.

443 MILLER, Shakespeare, Romeo and Juliet, the House in which Shakespeare was Born. 2.

444 ALBERTI, Vire de la ville de Berne, Dunker, Plan Prospectif d'une Grande Partie des Cantons de Lucerne. 3.

445 CARL DOLCE, Ecce Homo, Ruibalini, Trans figuration, etc. 6.

446 CAZENAVE, Apollon Jonant de la Lyre, etc. 9.

447 ALBERTI, Vue de la ville de Berne, Chavin, Lausanne en Suisse. 3.

448 RAFEE, Blue Bells, Freebairn, Science Turning the Lamp of Life, India proofs, etc. 3.

449 RAFFE, Aurora, Blue Bell, India proofs etc. 3.

450 STOCKS, Playmates, Sharp, The Newspaper, India proofs, etc. 3.

451 Willmore, The Brook, Artlett, Sabrina, India proofs, etc. 3.
452 Greatbach, The Daughter of Zion, The Alchemist Lecturing on the Elixir of Life, India proof, etc. 8.
453 Jukes, Crescent near Birmingham and the General Infirmary at Sheffield, etc. 6.
454 Sandly, View of Bethlem Pennsylvania, View of Miramichi and Gaspe Bay on the St. Lawrence, etc. 8.
455 Views of Ancient Towns, Siard, Alagoa ad Austrum, Salvador, Sinus Omnium Santoru, very fine. 4.
456 Paul Potter, a Rural Scene, Leonardi da Vinci, Modeftia et Vanitas, etc. 6.
457 Shaw, View on the Wisahiccon, Pennsylvania, and Norfolk, from Gosport, Virginia, etc. 11.
458 American Indians, colored. 6.
459 American Indians, colored. 6.
460 American Indians, colored. 6.
461 Sharpe, Palissy the Potter, India proof Stewart, Hide and Seek, etc. 3.
462 Armytage, Hagar and Ishmael, Raffe, Aurora, etc. 8.
468 Wilkie, The King at Holyrood, etc., India proofs. 2.
464 Velasquez, Portrait from the Dresden Gallery, fine, Vandyck, Sancta Virgo, etc. 8.
465 Jardien, Adam v Eve repris de leur peche, Bartolozzi, Le Massacre de Innocens, etc. 5.
466 Wheatley, Irish Cottagers Crossing a Brook, Cignani, Potiphar's Wife Enticing Joseph, proof before letters, etc. 7.
467 Jeniers, les Miseres de la Guerre, Canat, View of Pierced Island in the Gulf of St. Lawrence, etc. 11.
468 Bolswert, Rural Scene after Rubens, Wouvermans, L'Abreuvoir des Chasseurs, etc. 3.
469 Vanloo, St. Gregoire Obtient un Miracle a la Messe, Le Bas Vue de Santolict Village de Hollande. 2.
470 Dupuis, Predication de St. Jean, Le Bas, Adoration des Roys, etc. 6.

471 HORTEMELS, Mort d'Abel, Vallee, Mort di la Sainte
Vierge, etc.   8.

472 LE SUEUR, Empereur Henry IV aux pieds du
Pope Gregoire VII, La Calomnie peinte par
Apelles, etc.   4.

473 MOYREAU, Rebecca Le Sueur, Saint Sebastien, etc. 8.

474 RAVENET, Adoration des Bergers, Raimond, Jesus
Christ dans le Sepulcre, etc.   5.

475 PORTRAITS of Franz Snyder, Heinrich Liberti,
after Vandyck, etc.   6.

476 GERICKE, Portraits Dorothea Tabina, Cavalli
Hieronymo Grimano, etc.   3.

477 CANOT, View of Louisburg North America, Marc
Antoine, La Danse D'Armours, etc.   9.

478 CLAUDIA, St. Peter von Aleantara, The Ten Vir-
gins, etc.   6.

479 BROMLEY, Prints Illustrating the History of England.   11.

480 AMERICAN Indians, colored.   6.

481 DESPLACES, Le Calvaire, le Comte de C, La Mort
D'Adonis etc.   6.

482 JOEL, Persicha, grand decorations of the Vatican. 3.

483 JARDIEN, Jupiter et Alcmene, Lepicier, Jupiter
et Junon etc.   11.

484 DU FLOS, Les Disciples d'Emaus, after Paul
Veronese Audran, Galathee, very fine.   2.

485 RAVENET, La vie Humaine, Aubert, Mars et Venus
lies par l'Armour etc.   3.

486 EDELINCK, Portrait of Castiglione, Youllain, Mer-
cure et herse etc. fine pieces, good impressions. 9.

487 RAVENET, Venus et Adonis, Poilly, Jupiter et
Danae etc.   11.

488 ABRAHAM offering Isaac, and various Biblical subjects, fine Italian engravings.   14.

489 FLIPART, Christ in the Mount of Olives, Desplaces, Adoration of the Shepherds, fine, etc. 12.

490 PRIOR, Golden Horn India proof, Sharpe, The
Visit to Melancthon, India proof.   2.

491 LE GRAND, Mr. Vincent Boyer.   1.

492 VALEE, St Jean Baptiste, Chereau St. Jean dans
le Dexerz, very fine etc. 3.

493 RAPHAEL, Holy Family, very fine, Jardien, Noli
me tangere, etc. 3.

494 DOMENICHINO, Sibilla Cumana, fine. 1.

495 HACKERT, Vuc des Champs Phlegreens, and
Veduta di Pozzuoli, etc. 9.

496 LARMESSIN, Jardien etc , Illustrations to Milton
and Shakespeare, fine engravings. 9.

497 CHALLIS, Utrecht India proof, Sharpe, Youth and
Pleasure. 2.

498 PORTRAITS Illustrating the History of France. 50.

499 HANSSART, Illustrations to Milton and Shakspeare,
fine. 3.

500 DAULLE, Portrait of Joann Bapt. Coignard, very
fine. 1.

501 MURILLO, Beggar Boy, Beisson, Judith, etc., fine
pieces from Musee Francais. 3.

502 BOLSWERT, Pastoral Scenery after Rubens, Watteau, Fetes au Dieu Pan, etc. 6.

503 BAKER, Son of Niobe, fine India proof, au Hour
in the Park, etc. 13.

504 DOMENICHENO, Sibylla Cumaea, fine. 1.

505 LANFRANCUS, Peter Walking on the Sea, fine,
Poussin, Holy Family, etc. 10.

506 CUYPE, The Contented Peasant, Claude Lorrain,
La Fete Villageoise, etc. 6.

507 SHAW, Jones Falls near Baltimore, and View by
Moonlight, near Fayettville, N. Carolina, etc. 17.

508 CHALLE, La Mort D' Hercule, fine, etc. 3.

509 GUIDO, La Magaleine, the superb, engraving by
Lignon. 1.

510 THE HEAVENS are telling the Glory of God, etc. 3.

511 YUKES, View of the Fountain of Egeria near
Rome, etc. 4.

512 GALLE. The Crucifixion, very fine, Marci, Christ
presented to the Lord, etc. 4.

513 GALLE, Lifting up of the Brazen Serpent, very fine. 3.

514 BUST of Classical Authors and Coins by Ulmer,
Godfrey, etc. 12.

515 CANOT, View of Montreal, etc. 8.
516 REMBRANDT, Christ Raising the Widow's Son, proof before letters. 1.
517 GALLE, Virgin and Child, very fine, etc. 3.
518 RAPHAEL, La Transfiguration, Taking down from the Cross, etc. 4.
519 BAKER, Retrospection, Mola, The Tomb of our Savior, etc. 5.
520 BOLSWERT, Silenus, Rega, Le Bon Menage. 2.
521 BARTOLOZZI, Virgin and Child, etc. 3.
522 PORTRAITS Illustrating the History of France. 50.
523 AGOSTINO Caracci, Tobit and the Angel. Rare. 1.
524 TURNER, Portrait of Meerza, Jiafer, Jabeeb. Colored, etc. 7.
527 YUKES, Dover Castle, from the Beach, etc. 7.
528 SHAW, Lynnhaven Bay. Colored, etc. 6.
529 DARET, Accipe me Cupido dignam te Coniugem et tu Zephine, etc. 2
530 VIEWS of Gloucester Cathedral, Proof, National Gallery, London, etc. 6.
531 PORTRAITS Illustrating the History of France. 50.
532 VANLOO, Ænas Saving his Father, etc. 5.
533 LAWRENCE, Portrait of the Duke of Wellington, etc. 4.
534 WOUVERMANS, La Fontaine de Neptune, etc. 3.
535 RAPHAEL, Sainte Celcile. India proof, very fine, etc. 2.
536 DESANDRE, L'Imperatrice Eugenie et Son Fils. Coloured, etc. 3.
537 CHEREAU, Portrait of Nicolas de Launay. 1.
538 METZMACHER, Portrait of Philippe de Champaigne. 1.
539 SCHUVVEN, Portrait of Cardinal Candavo. Fine impressions. 1.
540 BUST of Classical Authors, and Coins by Cattini, Ghgi, etc. 20.
541 SCULPTURE Illustrating the History of France. 43.
542 AMERICAN Indians, colored. 6.

543 AMERICAN Indians, colored. 6.

544 AMERICAN Indians, colored. 6.

545 AMERICAN Indians, colored. 7.

546 BUST of Classical Authors and Coins, by Bossi, Fontana, etc. 10.

547 BUST of Classical Authors and Coins, by Mochetti, Carratteni, etc. 6.

518 RAPHAELIS, Amasia, vulgo La Fornarina, fine. 1.

549 SCOTT, Temple of Love,. and Peter the Hermit Preaching the Crusades, etc. 5.

550 GOODALL, The Ferry, fine. 1.

551 BOLSWERT, Entombing of Christ, very fine. 1.

552 SIR J. REYNOLDS, Mother and Child, proof before letters. 1.

553 METZU, Une Femme Tenant un pot de Biere. 1.

554 BOYDELL, The Power of Beauty, fine. 1.

555 GIUSEPPE Longhi, Entombing the Body of Christ, very fine. 1.

556 SWANNEVELT, Adonis carried of by Venus, fine. 1.

557 WOUVERMAN'S Pillage des Reitres, Occupations, Champestres. 2.

558 VASSEUR, L'Antomne, very fine, etc. 2.

559 PATER, A Champetre, etc., India proofs. 2.

560 ARMITAGE, Battle of Mecanee, etc., India proofs. 2.

561 GALLE, Christ bearing the Cross, and the Crucifixion, etc. 3.

562 TURNER, Venice, Orange Merchantman going to Peices, India proofs. 2.

563 THE River Bank, by J. Vander Hayden, India proofs. 2.

564 THE Horn, after Van de Weld, India proofs, etc. 2.

565 TURNER, Rome from the Vatican, Boats off Calais, India proofs. 2.

566 TURNER, Crossing the Brook, Peace Burial of Wilkie, India proofs. 2.

567 AMERICAN Indians, colored. 7.

568 AMERICAN Indians, colored. 7.

569 BACON, The Nymph of the Waterfall, India proof,
Wass The Blossoms. 2.

570 PORTRAITS Illustrating the History of France. 50.

571 TURNER, Norham Castle, Ancient Italy, India
proofs. 2.

572 TURNER, Stranded Vessel of Yarmouth, Decline
of Carthage, India proofs. 2.

573 TURNER, Venice, The Dogana, The Grand Canal
Venice, India proofs. 2.

574 VIEWS of Ancient Cities, Balo, Berne, Zuric, etc. 12.

575 LEWIS, Portrait of Lord Byron, fine. 1.

576 SHAKSPERE'S Birth Place, proof. 1.

577 AVELINE, La Belle Cuisiniere, after Boucher. 1.

578 PYE, A Land Storm, Heath, Lovers Quarrel, etc. 8.

579 ETCHING, by Goodall, Italian Scenery, Artist
proof, A young Painters first Work. 2.

580 ETCHING, by Rembrandt, Taking Down from the
Cross, original, very fine. 1.

581 ETCHING, by Tomkins, proof, The Last Supper. 1.

582 HOGARTH, Marriage A-la-Mode, Original impressions, scarce. 6.

583 ETCHINGS, by Castilionus Genovese, Heads on a
sheet, fine. 4.

584 ETCHINGS, by Hercau, Degeorge Lalunze, etc.,
Entre Triomphale au Village, etc. 8.

585 ETCHINES, by Leys, A Legras, etc., Interior de
Luther a Wittenberg, etc. 6.

586 ETCHINGS, by Cham, Laurens, etc., Le Lac Nemi
(Italie), etc. 6.

587 ETCHINGS, by Buret, Debames, etc., Views, etc. 7.

588 ETCHINGS, by Brendel, Vollon, Flameng, etc.,
Une Bergeri, etc. 7.

589 ETCHINGS, by Rembrandt, Queyroy, etc., Pontes,
etc. 7.

590 MARCHE D'Armee and Choc de Cavalerie, after
Wouverman. 2.

591 ETCHING, by Tomkins, The Resurrection. 1.

592 JAMES Dawkins and Robert Wood, first discovery
of Palmyra, after Hamilton. 1.

593 McArdell, Rubens with his Wife and Child, fine. 1.

594 Warren, Font in the Desert, Pater Fete Champetre, India proofs. 2.

594*Beauwarlet, Le Calin Maillard, fine impression after Fragonaut. 1.

595 Portraits of Generals U. S. Grant and P. H. Sheridan. 2.

596 Turner, Abingdon, Berkshire, Ulysses Deriding Polyphemus, India proofs. 2.

597 Turner, Brighton Chain Pier, Petworth Park, India proofs. 2.

598 Turner, The Loretta Necklace, Regulus leaving Carthage, India proofs. 2.

599 Turner, View of Orvieta, Hannibal Crossing the Alps, India proofs. 2.

600 Turner, Temple of Jupiter, Panhellenius, The Death of Nelson, India proofs. 2.

601 Turner, The Opening of the Walhalla, Dido Building Carthage, India proofs. 2.

602 Turner, The Battle of Trafalgur, The Lake of Lucerne, India proofs. 2.

602*A Literary Party of Sir Joshua Reynolds, India proof. 1.

603 Fuseli, Shakspeare, King Henry the Fifth. 2.

604 Hamilton, Shakspeare, Coriolanus, and Cymbeline. 2.

605 West, Shakspeare, As You Like It. 2.

606 Hodges, Shakspeare, As You Like It, and Merchant of Venice. 2.

607 Northcote and Stothard, Shakspeare, Othello, and King Henry VI. 2.

608 Tresham and Rigaud, Shakspeare, Antony and Cleopatra, and Comedy of Errors. 2.

609 Opie and Peters, Shakspeare, King Henry VIII, and Timon of Athens. 2.

610 Reynolds and Hamilton, Shakspeare, King Henry VI, and As You Like It. 2.

611 Romney and Lucebi, Shakspeare, Two Gentlemen of Verona, and Tempest. 2.

612 CHRIST and the Woman at the Well, fine old engraving. 1.
613 LES Petits Marodeurs after Morland, etc. 2.
614 HEADS of the Cæsars after Philips, on a sheet, fine. 8.
615 ADAM and Eve finding the Dead Body of Abel after Werff, very fine. 1.
616 GRIGNION, View of the Jesuits College and Church Scotin, River Manyfold at Wetten Hill, etc. 7.
617 PORTRAITS of Charles Sumner, Joseph Hume, Wilkie, Village Festival, etc. 7.
618 HOWARD, Una Coming to Seek the Assistance of Gloriana, etc. 9.
619 ROBERTS, Melrose Abbey, Portrait of Eliza Bacciochi, etc. 6.
620 WINSTANLEY, Amour Scientiarum after Vandyck, Woolnath, Joshua Commanding the Sun to Stand Still, etc. 5.
621 BETTELINI, Sibylla Persica after Barbieri, etc. 2.
622 ANDRAN, St Francis in ecstacy before the Sacrament, Rainaldi, Congiura di Cortiliana, etc. 4.
623 NORMAND, Noces de land, Dunkarten, Henry the Great of France and Navarre, etc. 6.
624 HAMILTON, Shakespeare, Twelfth Night, Love's Labor's Lost. 2.
625 SMIRKE, Shakespeare, Merry Wives of Windsor. 2.
626 SMIRKE, Shakespeare, King Henry the Fourth. 2.
627 KIRK, Shakespeare, Measure for Measure, and Titus Andronicus. 2.
628 WHEATLEY and Smirke, Shakespeare, All's well that ends well, and Taming the Shrew. 2.
629 PORTRAITS, Duke of Cambridge after Ross, proof, Bromley, Warren Hastings, etc. 4.
630 WESTALL, Shakespeare, Julius Cæsar, colored. 1.
631 NUDE Figure in Italian Oil by Lyons. 1.
632 SARTAIN, President William Henry Harrison, after Lambdin fine. 1.
633 NORTHCOTE, Shakespeare, King Richard, II and III. 1.
634 DOWNMAN, Shakespeare, As you like it. 2.

635 BARTOLOZZI and Ryder, Shakespeare, Twelfth
Night. 2.

636 WHEATLEY, and Opie, Shakespeare, Winter's Tale. 2.

637 BOURNE, The Village School, Godfrey. The
Tomb of Grace Darling, India proofs. 2.

638 ROLLS, Rebekah at the Well, Sherratt, The
Woman of Samaria, India proof. 2.

639 KNOLL, The Fortune Teller, Devachez, The Hin-
doo Maiden, India proofs. 2.

640 SHARPE, Critics, Brown, Our Pets, India proofs. 2.

641 ROLLS, The Way Side in Italy, Radclyffe, The
Homeward Bound, fine. 2.

642 PRIOR, The Council of Horses, Sharpe, A Baby
was Sleeping, India proofs. 2.

643 GREATBACH, The Riven Shield, Shaw, Cottage
Children, India proofs. 2.

644 WALLIS, The Scheldt Texel Island, Willmore,
Men of War at Sheerness, India proofs.

645 BOURNE, The Duel Interrupted, Greatbach, The
White Cockade, India proofs. 2.

546 DURNO, Shakespeare, Merry Wives of Windsor,
and King Henry the Fourth. 2.

647 WRIGHT, Shakespeare, Tempest and Winter's
Tales. 2.

648 ARMYTAGE, Battle of Mecanee, Hammersley, a
View from Bonn, India proofs before letters. 2.

649 PORTRAITS and Medals of Napoleon, Illustrating
his Life and Times. 49.

650 ARMYTAGE, The Sonnet, Cousen, a Hawking
Party, etc. 21.

651 PORTRAITS of Lord Palmerston, Gen. Sir J. F.
Burgoyne, Hon. and Rev. Baptist W. Noel. 20.

652 ALBERT DURER, St. Sebastian, and Jealousy, etc. 3.

653 LEYDEN, Eve tempted by the Serpent, Christ bearing the Cross, etc. 4.

654 LANDSEER, Combat, Artist proof, very fine. 1.

655 LANDSEER, Challenge, Artist proof, very fine. 1.

656 SIR WALTER Scott's Monument at Edinburgh,
fine folio. 1.

657 ETCHINGS by Smallfield, Clark, Langen, etc., Wild Boars, A Young Monkey, etc. 6.

658 ABRAHAM Offering up his Son Isaac, after Rembrandt, very fine. 1.

659 CHRIST Disputing with the Doctors after Rembrandt, splendid line engraving proof before letters. 1.

660 SHAKESPEARE, a Portrait on India paper, proof before letters very fine. 1.

661 ETUDE par Ruotte etc., La Vieillesse etc. 4.

662 FEMALES by Perrot, Bertrand, Cardon, etc., La Nuit, Mariee, Candeur etc. 4.

663 STATUARY by Whessell, Forster etc., Male Figures. 4.

664 CRAYON Drawing of the French Academy. 7.

665 ETUDE of Animals par Legrand, The Horse, Veau, Mule, etc. 4.

666 AVRIL, Cæsar Auguste, Viero, Portrait, etc. 3.

667 ETCHING Cupid and Pysche, Bourgeous, Jeune Russe, etc. 3.

668 RURAL Scenery, proofs before letters. 3.

669 STATUARY by Potrelle, Lange, Forster, The Archer, etc. 3.

670 COUSEN, The Harvest Cart, A Summer Moon, Hampton Court, etc. 20.

671 ETCHINGS by Carolus, Abraham, etc., Site en Narvege, Bards de L'Ondon, etc. 6.

672 ETCHINGS by Taiee, Montarlot, Laurens, etc. Marrons D'Inde, etc. 6.

673 ETCHINGS by Lalanue, Mar etc., A Meulan, Demolitions du Boulevard St Germain, etc. 4.

674 ETCHINGS by Cuvier, Cladel etc., Passage d'Italie, Lap Doge etc., India proofs. 4.

675 ETCHINGS by Debaines, Dupray, etc., Ruins de Chateau de Jancarville etc., India proofs. 4.

676 FEMALES by Sauve, Girard, Mecou etc., Attention Ecossaise, Estelle, etc. 5.

677 FEMALES by Bertrand, Perrot etc., Hermione, Chaperon Rouge, etc. 7.

678 ETUDE par Jazet, Coqueret, de Chevel Russe, Francais. 4.

679 LANDSCAPES, proofs before letters.   3.

680 STATUARY, Male Figures.   3.

681 GIRARD, Jeune Hollandaise; Massol, Jeune Espagnole, etc.   3.

682 GIRARD, La Toilette, Massol, Le Martin, etc.   3.

683 STATUARY, by Girard, Ruotti, etc., Clio, Polymnie, Euterpe, Thalie, etc., very fine.   8.

684 VIERA, Tacita siede, Coglie l'onare, etc.   3.

685 RUOTTE, La Magdeleine, Sauve, Le Souenir, etc.   8.

686 AMERICAN Portraits.   50.

687 THE Vintage in the South of France, Wood cutting in Windsor Forest, etc.   20.

688 THE Death of the Stag, by Landseer, The Riven Shield, etc.   20.

689 MARY washing the feet of Christ, Vestigia delle Terme di Tita, etc.   4.

690 PORTRAIT of Raphael, St. Francis Assi, etc.   3.

691 SHARPE, The Young Falconer, Stanfield, The Scheldt Texel Island, etc.   49.

692 PORTRAITS of George Washington.   25.

693 TINTERN Abbey, Moonlight on the Wye, Morning on the Nile, etc.   41.

694 PORTRAITS of Masaccio, Jesus Christ, after Titien.   2.

695 PORTRAIT of Carolus V, after Rubens, very fine.   1.

696 PORTRAITS of Gen. Sheridan and Lord Hill.   2.

697 AMERICAN and English Views.   50.

698 NAPOLEON, Portraits and scenes in his Life.   50.

699 PORTRAITS of Baron Von Humboldt, Sir John Lawrence, Lord Panmure, etc.   25.

700 FINE Steel Engravings Illus. Scripture History.   50.

701 SHAKSPEARE before Sir Thomas Lucy, and the House in which he was born.   2.

702 PSICHE PUNIE, Duclos Figure du Tombeau de Medicis, etc.   5.

703 PORTRAITS after Rembrandt, fine.   2.

704 VAN SCHUPPEN, Portrait of Baron de Marainville, very fine engraving.   1.

704 PRINTS Illustrating Scripture History.   50.

706 VIEWS Battles etc., Illustrating American History. 50.

707 PORTRAITS of Bp. Lee, Lord John Russell, Sir
John Franklin, etc. 20.

708 PORTRAITS of Richard Cobden, Rev. T. Binney,
Rob. Stevenson etc. 16.

709 PORTRAITS of the Earl of Carlisle, Sir John Pack-
ington, etc., large paper. 3.

711 PORTRAITS after Rembrandt. 3.

712 SHAKESPEARE Illustrations. 300.

713 AMERICAN Indians, Chiefs, colored and others,
curious. 36.

714 NAPOLEON, Portraits and Medals. 86.

715 THE Visit to Melancthon, The South Sea Bubble,
etc., Steel engravings. 40.

716 DREVET, Portrait of Joannes Palinier, fine line
engraving. 1.

717 CALLCOTT, Trent in the Tyrol, White, Gen. Marion
inviting a British Officer to Dinner, very fine. 2.

718 LEYDEN, Christ on the Mount of Olives, and the
Crucifixion, etc. 6.

719 SIR J. REYNOLDS, Prudence, Etchings, by Martial,
etc., very fine. 3.

720 CARICATURES, The Senses, colored. 11.

72I STEEL Portraits of Noblemen, etc. 187.

722 PORTRAITS of Sir Walter Scott. 19.

723 STRANGE, Rob., Zephyrus the West Wind, very fine. 1.

724 THE Descent from the Cross, and others, illustrating Scripture History. 83.

www.ingramcontent.com/pod-product-compliance
Lightning Source LLC
Chambersburg PA
CBHW021550270326

41930CB00008B/1448